this is my faith

Judaism

by Holly Wallace

Copyright © ticktock Entertainment Ltd 2006
First published in Great Britain in 2006 by ticktock Media Ltd.,
Unit 2, Orchard Business Centre, North Farm Road,
Tunbridge Wells, Kent, TN2 3XF

We would like to thank: Jean Coppendale, Honor Head, Plan UK and Plan International,
Jonathan Gorsky and John Keast

With special thanks to Yoni and his family

ISBN 978 1 84696 030 7
Printed in China
2 3 4 5 6 7 8 9 10

Picture credits
t = top, b = bottom, c = centre, l = left, r = right,
OFC = outside front cover, OBC = outside back cover

Alamy: 9t, 11b, 27b, 28b, 29t. Art Directors & Trip Photo Library: 9b, 25, 27c. Corbis: 12,13,
19b, 19c, 23t, 27t, 29b, 31b. Getty Images: 5t, 13, 23c. Shutterstock: 5c, 5b, 17t, 18b, 19t, 23b,
30t. Yoni Marcus: OFC,1, 2, 4b, 7t, 7b, 11t, 12b, 14b, 15t, 15b, 20b, 22b, 31t, OBC.

Every effort has been made to trace the copyright holders, and we apologize in advance for any
unintentional omissions. We would be pleased to insert the appropriate acknowledgements in any
subsequent edition of this publication.

Contents

I am a Jew 4-5

My family 6-7

LEARN MORE: What is Judaism? 8-9

What I believe 10-11

LEARN MORE: The holiest book 12-13

Where I worship 14-15

Worshipping at home 16-17

Holy days 18-19

Pesach 20-21

Hanukkah 22-23

Other festivals 24-25

Special occasions 26-27

LEARN MORE: Holy places 28-29

Glossary 30-31

Index 32

Words that appear in **bold** are explained in the glossary.

I am a Jew

"My name is Yoni Marcus. I am eleven years old and I live in New York in the USA. My family follow the religion of **Judaism**. This means that we are **Jews**."

"My religion is very important to me. It teaches me what is right and wrong and how people should live together. It is also a way to say what you think about life."

This is Yoni. Here he is wearing his red **kippah**.

The Star of David has been used as a symbol by Jewish people for over a thousand years.

"Jews often use a star with six points as a **symbol** for our religion. This star is called the Star of David and it represents the shape of **King David's** shield."

"The **menorah** is another Jewish symbol. It is a type of candlestick which holds seven candles."

This type of candlestick is kept in some synagogues but it is never lit. It is kept as a symbol of the Jewish people.

Jews wear a kippah when they pray to show respect to God.

"I always wear a small, round cap called a kippah when I pray. Some Jews wear a kippah all the time."

My family

"I live with my mother, father and an older sister. We live in a house in the middle of a busy city. My grandmother also lives in New York and I have grandparents in Israel."

"My mother is a rabbi so we do lots of Jewish things and talk about Judaism. A rabbi is someone who has studied Jewish history and ideas, and is like a teacher."

My father, Yigal.

This is me, Yoni.

Liya, my sister.

My mother, Hara.

The rules about kosher food are found in our holy book, the **Torah.** Keeping these rules is important for many Jews.

"At home we eat kosher food. This includes not eating pork and shellfish, and not eating dairy foods at the same time as meat."

"Before and after a meal, everyone says a short prayer to thank God for our food. On the **Shabbat**, we also light candles."

Yoni's mother says a blessing over the Shabbat candles after she lights them.

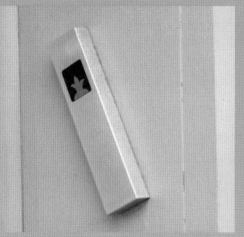

The mezuzah fixed to the doorframe of Yoni's house contains part of the holy **Shema prayer.**

"There is a **mezuzah** fixed to the doorpost of our house. We touch it every time we enter and leave as a sign of love for God."

LEARN MORE: What is Judaism?

- Judaism is one of the oldest religions in the world. The history of Judaism goes back a very long way, to the time of a man called **Abraham**. He lived in the Middle East more than 4,000 years ago. The people of Abraham's time worshipped many different gods and he did not agree with them. Instead, he taught the people to worship only one God. Abraham and his family became the first Jews.

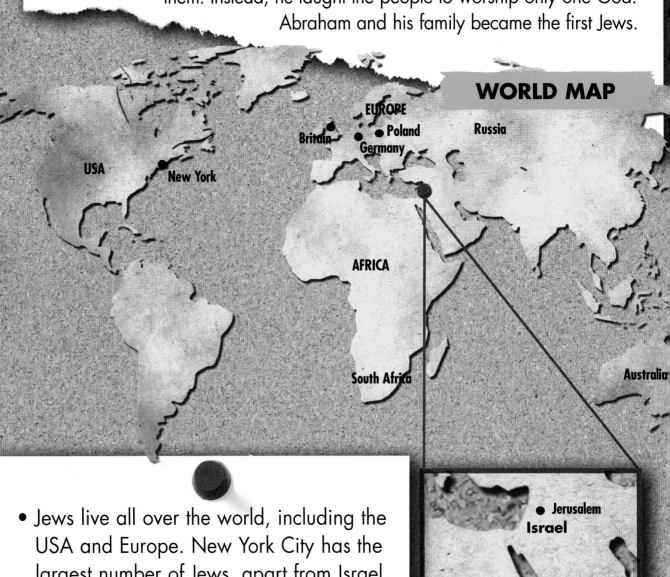

WORLD MAP

EUROPE
Britain
Germany
Poland
Russia

USA
New York

AFRICA

South Africa

Australia

Jerusalem
Israel

- Jews live all over the world, including the USA and Europe. New York City has the largest number of Jews, apart from Israel. Yoni has relatives in Britain, South Africa, Australia, Russia, Germany and Poland, but mostly in Israel.

- There are two main branches of Judaism. Orthodox Jews follow the ancient laws of Judaism. For Reform Jews the laws are a guide for how to live in the modern world. Yoni's family are Reform Jews.

Some synagogues, such as the Great Synagogue in Budapest, Hungary, are highly decorated, others are quite plain.

- The Jewish holy book is the **Hebrew Bible**, especially the first five books, called the Torah.

- Jews worship God in a **synagogue**. A synagogue can be built anywhere and any type of building is suitable.

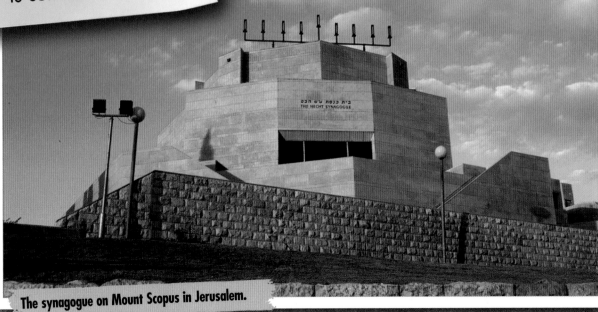

The synagogue on Mount Scopus in Jerusalem.

What I believe

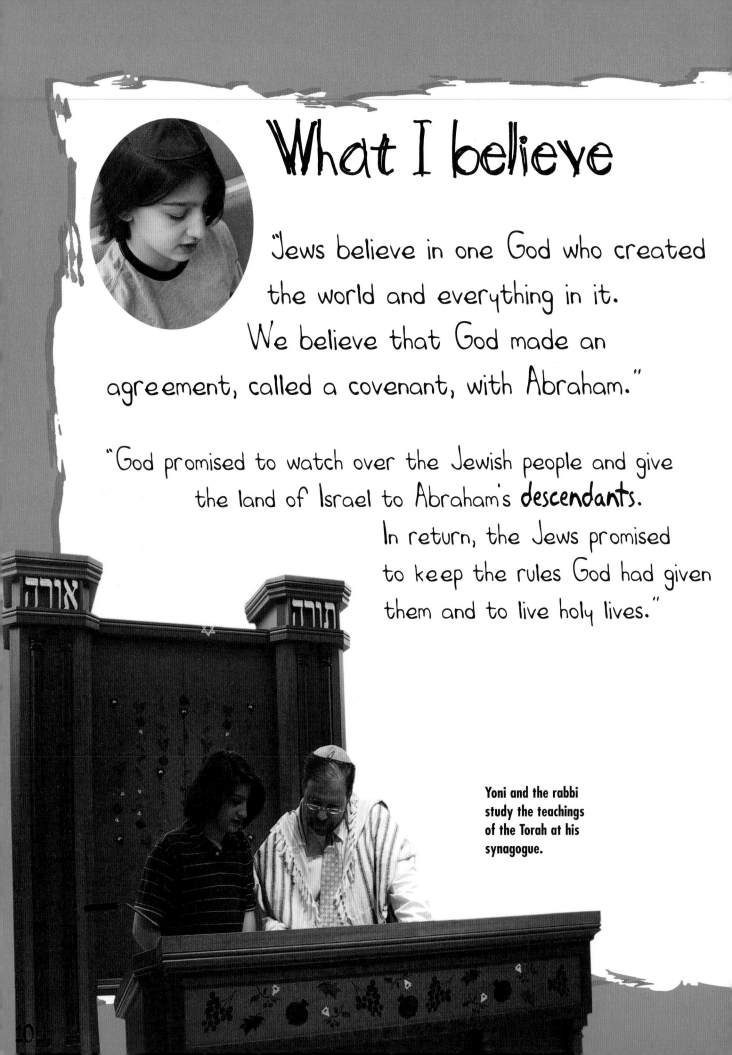

"Jews believe in one God who created the world and everything in it. We believe that God made an agreement, called a covenant, with Abraham."

"God promised to watch over the Jewish people and give the land of Israel to Abraham's **descendants**. In return, the Jews promised to keep the rules God had given them and to live holy lives."

Yoni and the rabbi study the teachings of the Torah at his synagogue.

The rabbi at Yoni's synagogue gets the Torah out of the Ark to be read.

"The Torah scrolls are kept at the front of the synagogue in a special cupboard called the Ark. The scrolls in my synagogue are wrapped in velvet."

"My religion teaches me to help others. I helped with one of my sister's projects which was to collect teddy bears for sick children."

Yoni and his family give toy teddy bears to children in hospital.

The Ten Commandments were handed down to **Moses** from God and are often on display in synagogues.

"I believe that the Ten Commandments are ten rules which God gave to the Jews, so they could live good lives."

LEARN MORE: *The holiest book*

• The holiest book for the Jews is the Hebrew Bible. It contains the Torah (the Five Books of Moses), the **Books of the Prophets** and the **Books of Writings**.

This picture shows two Torah scrolls in the Ark at the Brooklyn Heights synagogue. This is the holiest part of the synagogue.

• The words of the Torah are handwritten on scrolls in Hebrew. This is the ancient language of the Jews and also the language of the modern country of Israel.

- If a mistake is made when copying a scroll, the whole section must be removed and started again.

- The Torah teaches Jewish history and **traditions** and how to live a better life. It is read in the synagogue on Saturdays, Mondays and Thursdays.

These children are studying the Torah with a rabbi before they become **Bar** or **Bat Mitzvah**.

This picture shows the story of Esther written in Hebrew. "Esther" is one of the books in the Hebrew Bible.

- When a copy of the Torah becomes too old to read, it is not thrown away, but it is buried as a sign of respect.

Where I worship

"Once a week I go to the Brooklyn Heights Synagogue to worship. We pray and sing songs. On Shabbat, The Torah is read. Then the rabbi gives a talk. We say some prayers in English and some in Hebrew."

"There is usually a time during the service for silent prayer, when you can think about whatever you want."

The Brooklyn Heights Synagogue is in the middle of a row of houses.

The rabbi at Yoni's synagogue wears a tallit, or prayer shawl, as he leads worship in the synagogue.

"Some people wear a prayer shawl. This is to show that God is all around you and to help you feel God's embrace."

"Some Jews wear **tefillin**. These are leather boxes with straps so they can be tied to the forehead and left upper arm. They contain passages from the Torah."

Tefillin are worn to remind Jews to keep God's word close to their mind and heart.

At the synagogue school Yoni learns about the values and traditions of Judaism.

"I also go to religious school in the synagogue twice a week. Here I learn prayers, Jewish history and the Hebrew language."

Worshipping at home

"On Friday nights we celebrate the start of Shabbat which lasts from Friday evening to Saturday night. It is a day of rest and prayer and we see it as a gift from God."

"Our parents say a blessing over the wine and bread, and also say a blessing over us. Sometimes we have people over for dinner and that's always fun."

Yoni's mother lights candles to welcome the Shabbat.

Challah is a plaited loaf made specially for the Shabbat meal.

"At the meal there are always two loaves of challah. They remind us of the bread which God sent to our **ancestors** after their **escape from slavery** in Egypt."

"At the end of Shabbat, there is a ceremony called Havdalah. Blessings are said over a glass of wine, a box of spices and a special plaited candle."

To mark the end of Shabbat, Yoni holds a lit candle which has several wicks.

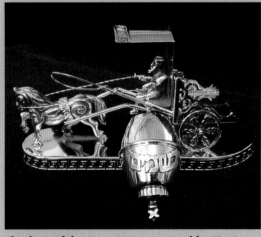

This beautiful spice container is used by Yoni's family at the end of Shabbat.

"Everyone sniffs spices such as cloves to carry the sweetness of Shabbat with them into the rest of the week."

Holy days

"The holiest days in the Jewish year are the Ten Days of Repentance. This is when we look back at the past year and say sorry for the bad things we have done."

"The Ten Days begin with the festival of Rosh Hashanah, the beginning of the Jewish year. The tenth day is called Yom Kippur. This is the holiest day in the year."

A ram's horn, called a shofar, is blown in synagogues to call Jews to repent, or ask for forgiveness, during Rosh Hashanah.

Eating apple dipped in honey is a Jewish tradition celebrating Rosh Hashanah.

"During Rosh Hashanah, Jews eat slices of apple dipped in honey to wish each other a sweet and happy new year."

"Yom Kippur usually takes place in late September or early October. On this day, Jews **fast** and spend time in the synagogue, praying and saying sorry to God."

Candles are lit during the evening service as a blessing.

During Sukkoth Jews collect and wave branches of palm, willow and myrtle trees and a citron fruit to thank God for food at harvest time.

"Five days after Yom Kippur is a festival called Sukkoth. This is when we remember how the Jews lived long ago, as they crossed the wilderness when they left Egypt."

Pesach

"There are many other important Jewish festivals. **Pesach** or Passover is a time when my whole family gets together including all my aunts, uncles and cousins. We have a big meal and remember how the Jews escaped from slavery in Egypt."

At the Pesach meal a plate of special food called a Seder plate is put on the table. On this plate are several different types of food which remind Jews of the sufferings and joys of the past.

Yoni's family and friends read the Haggaddah, the story of Passover, before they begin their meal.

"We always have spring onions with our meal which we dip into salt. This is to remind us of the bitter hardships of slavery and to be grateful for all that we have."

Hanukkah

"One of my favourite festivals is Hanukkah. The story of Hanukkah is great!"

"Long ago, the Jews won back the **Temple** in Jerusalem from their enemies. When they tried to light the Temple lamp, there was only enough oil for one day. But by a miracle, God kept the lamp burning for eight days, until new oil arrived."

Yoni and his family celebrate Hanukkah. This festival lasts for eight days and takes place in late November or December.

This is the candlestick that is lit during Hanukkah. The middle candle is used to light the other eight.

"We have a special candlestick with candles to represent the eight nights of Hanukkah. Each night we light a new candle and say blessings, until all the candles are lit."

"At Hanukkah we play a game called dreidl. You have to spin a top to win. The winner gets chocolate coins!"

During Hanukkah, Jewish families play games such as dreidl while candles are alight.

Latkes are cooked in oil. This oil is a symbol for the oil which burned in the ancient Jewish Temple lamp in Jerusalem and did not burn out.

"We eat lots of latkes, or fried potato pancakes, during Hanukkah. These are made from grated potato and onion mixed with flour and egg."

23

Other festivals

"We have many festivals. One of my favourites is Purim. This takes place between February and March. On this day we remember the story of Queen Esther who saved the Jews from being killed by an evil man called Haman."

"The best part of Purim is the play. Children act out the story of Esther and Haman at school or in the synagogue."

Many Jewish festivals involve a family meal. Yoni often helps prepare for visitors. Here he is polishing silver items to be used at the meal.

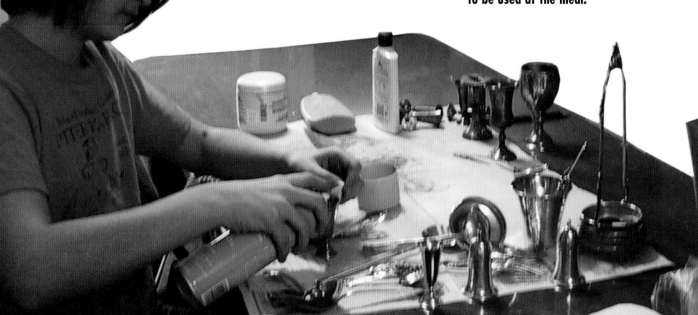

Children dress up in their favourite costumes to join in the story of Esther and Haman.

"Haman is the baddie who wanted to kill the Jews. When he comes on stage people boo and shout and make a loud noise with their rattles, called greggers."

"At Purim people also give each other small gifts, such as sweets or fruit. In Israel they have special street parades."

Each year in the city of Holon, in Israel, there is a big parade to celebrate the festival of Purim.

Shavuot is also a thanksgiving festival and is sometimes called the Festival of First Fruits.

"Another festival is Shavuot. This celebrates the time when God gave the Torah to Moses."

Special occasions

"Jews celebrate lots of special occasions and becoming Bar or Bat Mitzvah is one of the most important. This is when Jewish boys and girls take on adult responsibilities, such as leading a prayer service and reading from the Torah. They are also expected to follow other Jewish rules, such as fasting on Yom Kippur and helping the poor."

"My sister recently became Bat Mitzvah and we had a special service in the synagogue."

This is Liya, Yoni's sister, at her Bat Mitzvah. She is holding the Torah.

Once a boy or girl becomes Bar or Bat Mitzvah he or she can lead the service and read the Torah in the synagogue.

"For the Bar or Bat Mitzvah we have to choose a Mitzvah project where we do something to help others. I want to collect school books to give to Ethiopian children in Israel."

"At a wedding the bride and groom sign a marriage contract. The rabbi says blessings and the couple drink a cup of wine and exchange rings."

At a Jewish wedding the bride and groom stand under a canopy called a huppah. This stands for the new home that they both will share.

Many male Jews have the Star of David on their gravestone. Every year Jews light a candle to remember the person who has died.

"When someone dies there is a funeral service and a week of mourning. During the service, relatives read a prayer called the kaddish."

27

LEARN MORE: *Holy places*

- Israel is where the religion of Judaism started and this is where many of the most holy places are.

- The Temple in Jerusalem was the centre of Jewish worship and pilgrimage. In AD 70, Roman legions destroyed the city including the Temple, which was set on fire. The Western Wall is the only part that remains of the Temple. For Jews this is the holiest place on Earth.

Today millions of Jews visit the Western Wall to pray and many Jewish boys hold their Bar Mitzvah services here.

- The Western Wall is a centre of prayer and is visited by **pilgrims** from all over the world. Every day many Jews place prayers on small pieces of paper into the cracks in the Wall.

Mount Sinai is 2,400 metres high.

• This picture shows Mount Sinai. It is in the Sinai Desert, in Egypt. This is where Jews believe God gave Moses the Ten Commandments.

• Jerusalem was the ancient capital of Israel and it is also the modern capital. Most Jews think of Jerusalem as being at the centre of Jewish history and religion.

The city of Jerusalem attracts many tourists and pilgrims. The part which is known as the 'old city' is surrounded by walls.

Glossary

Kippot

Abraham The name Abraham means 'father of many' and Jews usually think of Abraham as the 'father' of the Jewish people.

Ancestors Family members who lived a long time ago.

Bar / Bat Mitzvah When a Jewish boy or girl is considered to be an adult by the synagogue. They are expected to obey the rules of Judaism.

Books of the Prophets Jews believe that the twenty-one books in this part of the Hebrew Bible are God's word, passed on to the Jews by the prophets

Books of Writings A collection of books included in the Hebrew Bible. Jews believe they were written by people who were filled with the Holy Spirit to produce great and holy works.

Descendants A person's family which comes after them.

Escape from Slavery Early in their history the Jews were slaves in Egypt. They were treated harshly. At Passover, Jews give thanks to God for putting an end to their suffering and setting them free. Their escape from Egypt is called the Exodus.

Fast To go without food, especially during a religious festival.

Hebrew Bible A collection of different books which some Jews believe are the word of God. This is known as the Old Testament by Christians. Hebrew is the ancient language of the Jews and also the modern language of Israel.

Jew Someone who is born of a Jewish mother. Some Jewish communities accept a child as Jewish if just the father is Jewish.

Judaism The religion of the Jewish people.

King David A great Jewish king of ancient times.

Kippah A small cap which Jews wear for worship in the synagogue. Some Jews wear a kippah all the time. The plural is kippot.

Menorah A candlestick that holds seven candles. It is a Jewish symbol.

Mezuzah The word 'mezuzah' means 'doorpost'. A mezuzah is fixed on the right side of the door in a Jewish home. It shows that the people of the house follow the word of God and the Torah.

Star of David

Mezuzah

Moses A great Jewish prophet. Jews believe that Moses received the Ten Commandments from God and led the Jews out of slavery in Egypt.

Pesach This is the Jewish word for Passover. This is the day when Jews remember how in ancient times they were saved from slavery in Egypt.

Pilgrims People who go on special journeys to visit holy places.

Prophet A person who passes on the word of God and who may often say what will happen in the future.

Shabbat The Jewish holy day of rest and prayer. It lasts from Friday evening to Saturday evening.

Shema prayer The most holy and important prayer in Judaism. It is also the first prayer a Jewish child is taught.

Symbol An object or sign that has a special meaning and that stands for something else.

Synagogue A building in which Jews meet to worship and study.

Tefillin Leather boxes with straps to attach them to the forehead and upper part of the left arm.

Temple The Temple in Jerusalem was a centre for Jewish prayer and pilgrimage. The First Temple built by King Solomon, a Jewish king, was destroyed by the Babylonians, an ancient group of people who were the Jews' enemies. The Second Temple was destroyed by the Romans in AD 70.

Torah Torah is the Hebrew word for the first five books of the Bible. These are also called the Five Books of Moses as Jews believe they were written by him.

Traditions Ways of doing something or beliefs that are passed down through families.

The scroll of Esther is written in Hebrew

31

Index

A
Abraham 8, 10, 30
ancestors 17, 30
Ark 11

B
Bar/Bat Mitzvah 13, 26–28, 30
beliefs 10–11
Bible 9, 12, 30
blessings 16, 23, 27
Books of the Prophets 12, 30
Books of Writings 12, 30

C
candles 5, 16, 17, 19, 23, 27
challah 17
covenant 10

D
descendants 10, 30
dreidl 23

E
escape from slavery 17, 30

F
family 6–7, 20
fasting 26, 30
festivals 19, 20–21, 22–25
food 7, 17, 19, 20–21, 23
Friday 16
funerals 27

G
God 7, 10–11, 16, 19

H
Haggaddah 21
Haman 24–25
Hanukkah 22–23

Hebrew Bible 9, 12, 30
Hebrew language 12, 14, 15
history 13, 15
holy days 18–19
holy places 28–29
huppah 27

I
Israel 6, 8, 12, 25, 28

J
Jerusalem 22, 28–29, 31
Jews, meaning 4, 30
Judaism, meaning 4, 8–9, 30

K
kaddish 27
King David 5, 30
kippah 4, 5, 30
kosher food 7

M
menorah 5, 30
mezuzah 7, 30
Middle East 8
Moses 25, 29, 30
Mount Sinai 29

O
Orthodox Jews 9

P
Passover 20–21
Pesach 20–21, 31
pilgrimage 28
prayers 7, 14, 16, 19, 27, 28, 31
prophets 31
Purim 24–25

Q
Queen Esther 24–25

R
rabbis 6, 14, 27
Reform Jews 9
Rosh Hashanah 18–19

S
Seder plate 20
Shabbat 7, 16–17, 31
Shavuot 25
Shema prayer 7, 31
shofar 18
slavery in Egypt 17, 20–21, 30
special occasions 26–27
Star of David 5, 27
Sukkoth 19
symbols 5, 23, 31
synagogues 9, 14–15, 31

T
tallit 15
tefillin 15, 31
Temple in Jerusalem 22, 28, 31
Ten Commandments 11, 29
Ten Days of Repentance 18
Torah 9, 11, 12–13, 14–15, 25, 26, 31
traditions 13, 31

W
weddings 27
Western Wall 28
wilderness 19
worship 14–15, 16–17

Y
Yom Kippur 18–19, 26